USBORNE FIRST
Level Two

renew by date shown.

There Was A Crooked Man
Retold by Russell Punter
Illustrated by David Semple

Susanna Davidson
Illustrated by Rocío Martínez

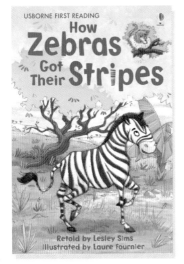

USBORNE FIRST READING
How Zebras Got Their Stripes
Retold by Lesley Sims
Illustrated by Laure Fournier

USBORNE FIRST READING
King Donkey Ears
Retold by Lesley Sims
Illustrated by Mike and Carl Gordon

Old Mother Hubbard

Retold by Russell Punter

Illustrated by Fred Blunt

Reading consultant: Alison Kelly
Roehampton University

Old Mother Hubbard
went to the cupboard,

to fetch her poor doggie
a bone.

But when she got there,
the cupboard was bare.

And so the poor doggie
had none.

Old Mother Hubbard
shut up the cupboard

and put on her warm
winter clothes.

"We'll have to go out," she said with a shout,

"before all the butchers
are closed."

So off down the lane,
through wind and
through rain,

went Old Mother
Hubbard and Spot.

'Til they came to a stop,
at Bob's Butcher's Shop.

And they went in to see
what was what.

Bob the Butcher

There was plenty of meat, for a doggie-sized treat,

but the old lady picked
out a bone.

Then came the snag,
when she looked in
her bag –

she had left all her
money at home.

The pair stepped outside.
"Stop thief!" came
Bob's cry.

Bob the Butch

And a man hurried by
in a flash.

He ran with such
speed, he tripped on
Spot's lead.

And went flying, along
with the cash.

"Your dog stopped that thief," said Bob with relief.

Bob the Butche

"So I must reward you, my dear."

Now Old Mother
Hubbard has a very
full cupboard.

And her doggie has
best steak all year.

Puzzles

Puzzle 1

Can you spot the differences
between these two pictures?
There are six to find.

Puzzle 2
Find these things in
the picture:

dog   clock   cupboard

window   cup   kettle

Puzzle 3

Choose the best sentence for each picture.

Answers to puzzles

Puzzle 1

Puzzle 2

clock   cupboard   window

kettle   cup   dog

Puzzle 3

I'm wet.

Stop thief!

Series editor: Lesley Sims

First published in 2010 by Usborne Publishing Ltd., Usborne House,
83-85 Saffron Hill, London EC1N 8RT, England. www.usborne.com
Copyright © 2010 Usborne Publishing Ltd.

All rights reserved. No part of this publication may be reproduced,
stored in a retrieval system or transmitted in any form or by any
means, electronic, mechanical, photocopying, recording or otherwise,
without the prior permission of the publisher. The name Usborne
and the devices 🔭 🎈 are Trade Marks of Usborne Publishing Ltd.
UE. First published in America in 2010.